W9-BXW-359

# 101 Media and Marketing Tips for the Sole Proprietor

Nanette Miner, MS

BVC Publishing
Bristol, Connecticut, USA

101 Media and Marketing Tips for the Sole Proprietor

By: Nanette Miner, MS
Cover Design: Red Barn Studios
(860) 267-6464

Published by:
BVC Publishing
P.O. Box 1819
Bristol, CT 06011-1819
USA

All rights reserved. No part of this book may be reproduced or transmitted in any form, or by any means, electronic or mechanical, including photocopying, recording or by any information storage and retrieval system without written permission by the publisher, except for the inclusion of brief quotations in a review.

Copyright © 1998, 1999 by BVC Publishing
ISBN 0-9650666-2-2
$7.95

**Attention Career Agencies, Professional Organizations and Trade Associations:**

Quantity discounts are available on bulk purchases (10 or more) of this book for educational purposes, fund raising, or gift givin

_____ *Table of Contents*

## ◄ Acknowledgments ►

Thanks go to my professional colleagues who contributed ideas, proofread and edited early editions, and encouraged the creation of this book: Marge Brown, Richard Beaty, Chris DeVany, Julie Hartland, Thomas Leonard, Temple Porter, and Joanne Schlosser.

## ◁ Preface ▷

Why is this book titled 101 Media and Marketing Tips for the *Sole Proprietor*? Because of the reality of every sole proprietor: you do almost all - if not all - of the work yourself, and you are on a limited budget. Every tip provided herein keeps those two realities in mind. When choosing which tips to include and which to leave out, the included tips had to meet four criteria:

1. They could not take forever to accomplish. Usually idea to fruition can be accomplished within a week - many times within a day; some take less than an hour.

2. They could not cost more than $500 to implement - most cost under $100.

3. They had to be *relationship* oriented and not sales oriented.

4. They had to be professional in appearance and execution.

This book is intended to help the sole proprietor establish visibility and credibility and to enhance marketability. As a bonus, sales will come.

# NETWORKING

## Tip #1      How to Network

Networking is unequivocally <u>the</u> most valuable business tool the sole proprietor can possess. I frequently say, "If I had better understood <u>how</u> <u>to</u> network when I first went into business for myself, I'd be a lot further along than I am." Networking allows you to make potential business connections in a non-sales way.

Three keys to becoming a successful networker:

1. Join associations (professional, community) and become active. Volunteer. Don't wait for "them" to come to you. Walk right up to the president of the group or a committee chair and say "How can I help?"

2. When faced with a room of strangers, act as if <u>you</u> are the host/hostess. Introduce yourself to others; introduce your new acquaintance to others. This becomes much easier when you've taken step one; now you can approach people and say, "Hi. I'm Chris. I'm on the membership committee..."

3. Encourage others to speak about themselves. Express an active interest in others. Don't dominate the conversation with what you do - it can come across as a sales pitch.

## Tip #2          Chambers of Commerce

Chambers of Commerce are one of the best ways to meet the "movers and shakers" in your community. Network with other managers, officers, and CEO's of the businesses in your area. If you live in an area that doesn't have a large enough business community to support a chamber, or perhaps the area business community isn't really your "target market," join the chamber of commerce from a neighboring community. Many people mistakenly believe that if they work in X-town they can only join the X-town chamber. Not true! Pick the association that's going to do the most for you.

## Tip #3          Professional Associations

There are thousands of professional associations out there, from human resource professionals, to retailers, to advertising agents and salespeople, to manufacturers ... the list goes on and on. It's easy to waste money by joining too many associations or joining the wrong ones. Be sure you thoroughly understand the association's purpose and the benefits of joining. Be selective, start with two or three associations and visit a few times as a guest. Get a feel for the members, the types of programs, and the benefits your membership would give you.

# Tip #4          Professional Associations, cont.

Belonging to a professional association is not some magical panacea that somehow brings you business.  Being able to state, "Member of _____" rarely causes the new customer to shout, "All right!  Sign me up!"  Once you join a professional association, be prepared to work for it.  Volunteer to do what needs to be done - big or small.  Do every task professionally and personably.  The more you do, the better you will be known and the more likely your name will spring to people's minds when they are asked to refer a person that does the type of work that you do.

# Tip #5          Non-professional associations

As many professional associations as there are, there are just as many associations that have no professional affiliation at all.  Individuals and business people from all walks of life join for the networking opportunities.  Associations of the self-employed, home-based business people, business networking groups and individuals looking to make a career change abound.  Check your local newspaper "community" listings for when and where these groups meet.

# Tip #6          Start Your Own Association

Can't find an association that meets your needs?  Start your own!  Use the newspaper and local radio to announce "Free!  The first meeting of the _____ will gather on _____ at _____.  All _____ are invited to attend."
One of the benefits of starting your own association is, that as the founder and contact person, everybody wants to meet you.  You can quickly establish a database of individuals with the same needs and purpose as your own.

## Tip #7          Job Fairs/Career Fairs

Many individuals mistakenly view a job fair or career fair as a place to go to get jobs. Au contraire - job fairs are a great place to go to sell jobs. If the local manufacturer's association is holding a job fair to recruit machinists, and you have a product or service that is useful to manufacturers, attend the job fair! Bring your marketing materials and a 60 second (or less) "pitch." Chances are you won't meet the exact individual that you need to speak with, but you will have made a personal association and have had an "insider" tell you who the appropriate contact should be.

## Tip #8          Team 100

Develop a list of 100 associates, colleagues and friends. Spend 90 days meeting-and-eating with each of them. Book breakfast and lunch meetings. Spend 30 minutes to an hour briefly speaking about what it is that you do, who your target market is, and how you benefit that market. Ask your contact to refer you whenever s/he meets a potential customer. Ask if you can help the contact in any way. Thank them for their time. Pay for the meal!

# Tip #9          Presentations to Civic Clubs

Civic organizations are constantly looking for presenters for their weekly or monthly meetings. Organizations such as the Rotary club, Kawanis club, Lion's club, women's club, and garden club can benefit from your expertise. Notice their meeting announcements in the newspaper and contact the person who is given as the club-contact. Offer to speak. You'll rarely be turned down and you'll be able to contact and impress 15 or more people at a time. Now that's an effective "sales" call!

# Tip #10          Business Expos

Many chambers of commerce hold yearly business expos. You don't always have to be a member of the chamber to have a booth at their expo. In addition, most major metropolitan areas hold annual home shows, auto shows, food shows, and bridal expos. What audience is most likely to need what you are selling? Contact the hosting organization or the event management company that is producing the show to find out how you can purchase a booth to display your wares and services. Be sure to make your booth attractive. Add balloons or a magician, or hold a raffle that will draw people to you.

# Tip #11          Referral Fees

Who would you most likely refer business to - a colleague that didn't thank you, or a colleague that did? How about a colleague that gave you a 10% or 20% referral fee, or a gift certificate for dinner? Now put the shoe on the other foot - let your associates, colleagues, and friends know that you will gladly compensate them for any referral that turns into business.

## Tip #12  Friends and Family Discount

Depending on the product or service that you promote, you may find the
"friends and family discount" to be the only marketing plan you need! Do you
install carpeting or detail cars? Are you a bookkeeper or a dry cleaner?
Offering 10% or $10 off your services is enough incentive for many, many
individuals to bring their business to you.

## Tip #13  Forget Your Cards

When networking with new associates, sometimes it's a good idea to "forget"
your cards back at the office. You can then collect the other person's card and
send them a short note the next day mentioning how much you enjoyed
meeting them, and enclosing your card. Marketing material might be
mentioned as, "I'm sending a few samples so that you can see the _____."
Because the person might have met six new people at the networking function,
you can easily get lost in the crowd. But how many of the six will send a
personal note the next day? Don't forget to include your card!

## Tip #14          Ask What You Can Do

There is a lot of truth to the saying, "It is better to give than to receive." When entering into any networking opportunity: professional association, chamber of commerce, spouse's company picnic - do not think of yourself and what you can <u>get</u> through your interaction with others - but, rather, think of what you can <u>give</u> to others. You'll find that what you give frequently comes back to you exponentially.

## Tip #15          Competition?  What competition?

Don't see your competitors as competitors - view them as collaborators. What do you provide that they don't, and vice versa? How can you help your customers by introducing them to your competitor and how can s/he do the same? Do you need a shorter lead time than your competitor? Can you provide smaller quantities or make house calls? Work out a mutually beneficial agreement to provide those products or services that your competitor cannot, and vice versa.

# GIFTS, GIMMICKS & GIVEAWAYS

**Tip #16**　　　　**You're a Life Saver!**

When someone does something you are thankful for or has gone above the call of duty, send them a small, padded Jiffy envelope with a roll of Lifesavers and a note that says:

> "Thanks! You were a lifesaver!"

**Tip #17**　　　　**Audio Tapes**

Audio tapes are attention getting and useful. They can be relaxing (music or nature sounds), humorous (classic comedy albums), or business oriented. Audio tapes are inexpensive (under $20) and can be purchased at any major book store, or subscribe to an audio book club and buy them ahead of time. Give them to new clients as a thank you, "old" clients as a way to keep in touch, or as a gift to all clients at holiday time.

**Tip #18**　　　　**Good Morning!**

If you have a local client base that consists of a group, such as a salesforce or small office, purchase personalized "doughnut boxes" and fill them with doughnuts. Deliver to the client personally or via a messenger. Deliver them once a week or once a month. Be consistent.

## Tip #19    And The Winner Is!

Hold a raffle.  Mail 1/2 of a raffle ticket to your customer with a short note explaining the gift and the drawing date.  Raffle tickets are inexpensive and can be purchased at any party supply store.  The prize doesn't have to be expensive - a mug, a pen and pencil set, or free (your product or service).  The raffle gives you an opportunity to contact all of your customers and to make one of them feel extra special.

## Tip #20    Compliments Of...

Put a specialty item (pen, toy, Post-it® note) in the event bag of the school science fair, the local college's technology fair, or local business expo.  It's cheaper than having your own booth, and you're assured that <u>everybody</u> that attends has your marketing item.

## Tip #21    Stick it!

Give away funny or poignant Post-It™ Notes.  They can be purchased at all office supply stores and through the Successories® catalog.  Post-It™ Notes come in single pack sizes of 80 sheets or cubes of almost 700 sheets.  Each time your recipient uses the notes - she will think of you.

## Tip #22          Pre-Paid Phone Cards

Pre-paid phone cards are handy to have around and a welcomed gift. Successories® stores and catalogs carry phone cards with inspirational messages on them. You can also purchase them with sports teams' names and logos, or other personal influences, which you can mix and match to your customers' personalities.

# DATABASES / MAILING LISTS

### Tip #23       Databases & Mailing Lists

Before you spend money on purchasing a database or mailing list, be very sure about who your target audience is and why you are contacting them. Purchase the "right" list for your needs and make sure that the list vendor has "cleaned" it in the last six months. Most lists only allow you one-time use - you don't want to waste it.

### Tip #24       Targeting Databases & Mailing Lists

You don't have to purchase an entire list if part of the list will meet your needs. Let's say that you are marketing a home radon testing kit. You've decided that the type of person who would purchase this kit is likely to be a "handyman." You contact the list owner of a popular home repair publication. You know that radon seeps in from the ground and only appears in basements in large enough quantities for the kit to detect. Although there is a large population of subscribers for the home repair publication in Georgia, Virginia and Florida - you don't need these names because most of them will not have basements.

Think of other ways you can eliminate groups of people from the list so that you can keep your costs down and your target market narrow.

## Tip #25　　　　List Brokers

List brokers will help you to narrow down your choices regarding who you need to target, where they are likely to be found, and what they are likely to be interested in. The broker makes a commission by selling the list to you. It behooves the broker to give you a list that works so that you will return in the future to buy the list again, or to purchase a different list. Think of the list broker as a consultant and use all of the services that s/he can give you.

## Tip #26　　　　One Time Use

You may not purchase a mailing list, you may only rent them. The list perpetually belongs to the list owner. Mailing list rentals run between 4 cents and 10 cents per name and allow you one time use. The list owner will "salt" the list with names that will return to him. In this way the list owner can be sure of your honesty in using the list only once. If they receive a second mailing from you - and you only paid to use the list once - expect to receive another bill in the mail.

## Tip #27　　　　Create Your Own List

The longer you are in business, the more contacts and customers you will collect. Before you rent somebody else's list, be sure to maximize the use of your own list. It's easy to print mailing labels and personalized letters to your own list via Mail Merge in Word, Avery Labels, or ACT!

## Tip #28          Offer (or sell) Your List

You need to have a rather extensive personal list (5,000+ names) before a list broker will represent you. But there are ways to use your list in your own community. What colleagues or clients would benefit from your list? Would you be willing to include a short note of introduction so that their mailing is well received? You may choose to give your list to a colleague or client in exchange for their list or for some other consideration; you may even choose to sell it. If you sell your list, charge at least 25 cents per name - remember, this is a small and highly targeted list, and you are endorsing the person who is using it. It is worth the higher per-person price.

## Tip #29          Formatting Your Own Mailing List

If you choose to create and market your own list, you need to save it in an ASCII format so that it can be read by any other database program. This allows your customer to use the list without having the same software program that
you do.

# INTERNET

### Tip #30          Web Page Design

Virtually everyone and his brother will tell you that they can design a web page. And it's probably true.  The quality of the page will be questionable, however. You can attempt to design your own by downloading Hot Dog or AngelFire from the Internet and following the step by step instructions.  In addition, there are web design software packages available for under $50.00 at office supply stores.

### Tip #31          Web Page Hosting

In addition to having a web page created, it must be hosted, or stored, on an Internet server.  Hosting services can range from $29 per month to over $100 per month depending on how much space you need, among other things. Check into your professional associations to see if they offer web page hosting. Yes, listing your page with your colleagues' pages increases your competition, but on the other hand, if someone is looking for your service they have a much better chance of finding the association page than they do in finding your individual page.  In addition, your association will more than likely do a lot more PR than you'll be able to do on your own, hence attracting people to your page.

For free hosting, CompuServe offers 5k of space on its server to any CompuServe member.

## Tip #32          Market Your Services via Other Web Pages

There are a number of organizations that have web pages solely dedicated to marketing your services.  These pages are especially useful for sole proprietors such as consultants, writers, editors, and IT professionals.  Anyone can fill out an on-line form and add their services and credentials to the list of available resources.  Check out:

> www.cvp.com/freelance
>
> www.eureka.it/freelance
>
> www.mbnet.mb.ca/f-pro

## Tip #33          Gaining Web Site Exposure

According to an American Internet User Survey, 21% (over 40 million) of U.S. adults are now on-line.  That is a one third increase over the second quarter of 1997.  The World Wide Web is destined to be as popular as television, and far more useful.

It is unlikely that your Web site will be a business success, unless you are also an expert in how to get exposure for your Web site.  There are millions of Web sites, all competing for attention from the on-line public.  You need to register your site with the available search engines if you hope to have anyone find you at all.  There are services that will do this for you at very reasonable rates, but be cautious.  Unless that company has been involved in the design of the Web site, it is unlikely that they understand how to position your product or service.  Be sure that you choose the key words that your customers will be likely to use to search for you.  Create a list of 20 key words.  For instance, if you sell a product that is dog related, likely words are: dog, pet, animal, canine, puppy, etc.

## Tip #34        Domain Name

Your address on the World Wide Web is important to your success.  All web addresses start with a domain name.  Your web site address can be part of someone else's domain, such as: "www.vtinet.com/yourcompany".  Or you can have your own domain name: "www.yourcompany.com".

Having your own domain name obviously shortens your web address and better identifies the site with your company.  But there are more important advantages than that.  One advantage is that you may dramatically improve your exposure through better positioning on web site search engines.  Just having your own domain name does not guarantee good positioning on search engines, but in certain cases, it is next to impossible to get good positioning without it.

It is getting extremely difficult to get a desirable domain name.  The rush to register relevant domain names means that it is getting increasingly unlikely that your first choice for domain name will be available.  This situation will only worsen as time goes on.

Even if you don't plan to open a web site now, you should register your choice of domain name and reserve it for when you are ready.  Domain name registrations cost only $100.00 with a possible service fee of usually less than $50.00 from the service company handling your registration.

## Tip #35        Promote Your Web Site Everyday

Make sure that your web address appears at the bottom of your e-mail messages, on your letterhead, and on all of your marketing materials and business cards.

# NEWSLETTERS

## Tip #36          Make It Eye-catching

You want your newsletter to be eye-catching.  Unique design, sharp graphics, photos or cartoons, snappy name or title.  Microsoft Publisher® allows you to create extremely eye-catching formats from your own computer and laser printer and with a minimal amount of work.  The software costs under $90 and can be found on sale for under $50.

## Tip #37          Make It Eye-catching, cont.

Hire a graphic artist to design a unique and colorful header (the upper 1-2 inches of the page) and format for your newsletter.  Use this design as a master - take it to a print shop and have hundreds or thousands of the master made up.  Each month (or quarter), format the newsletter on your computer, then run a stack of masters through your laser printer.  It looks as though it is custom printed each month and you save a lot of money by having the master duplicated en-mass.

## Tip #38          Write When The Mood Strikes You

Too often I've had a good idea for inclusion in my "next" newsletter, but when the time comes to write the next newsletter, I've forgotten what it was; even if I've written myself a note, I'm not as fervent about the thought as I was at the time it came to me.  Write when the inspiration strikes.  Write your newsletter three or six months in advance if you're able.  When the deadline looms to send the newsletter out you'll be thankful that all you need to do is print and mail.

## Tip #39          Mailing Your Newsletter

Remember that database of colleagues, clients, and friends you created? Start by mailing your newsletter to them. Ask for a referral on each newsletter - include an area that asks: "Do you know someone who could benefit from this newsletter? Please let us know who they are!" and include a space for them to fill out the contact's information. Set this area off with a border or some other eye-catching design.

## Tip #40          Faxing Your Newsletter

Be aware that every business person gets upwards of 5 newsletters a month (from their professional associations, their bank, the office supply store, their vendors, etc.). Yours must be unique and valuable for them to take the time to open the envelope and read it. Conversely, a brief, faxed newsletter usually gets read the day it arrives. Why? A fax implies some urgency. Also, because it is brief (one to two pages), the recipient can usually skim it while walking from the fax back to his/her desk.

## Tip #41          Grab Their Attention

David Letterman made Top 10 lists popular. Virtually everybody loves them. We also love:

"The 5 Reasons Why..."

"The 7 Secrets Of..."

"3 Things You Must..."

The point is - numbered lists work. So do questions. Start your articles off with compelling questions or statements such as:

"Do You Know Why Nearly Half of Your..." or

"Recent Research Reveals..."

## Tip #42          Postcard Newsletters

Postcards are so useful and versatile that the entire next chapter has been devoted to them. A postcard newsletter is sure to be read because it is short. It's also easy to write because ... it is short. You must limit yourself to one or two major ideas because that is all that will fit. The recipient reads it before she even realizes it because it is easy to glance at a 3x5 card and absorb the information.

## Tip #43          Create a Series

If you have a lot of information on a topic, create a series out of it. Reading a series is akin to reading a book - you can't wait to get to the next chapter to see what happens. Herald the next chapter by "teasing" your audience, "Next month we'll look at..." You can gain audience involvement by asking for responses to No. 1 in the series and reporting on the responses in the next edition of your newsletter.

# POSTCARDS

### Tip #44          Postcards

A postcard has immediate impact on the reader.  You don't have to depend on the reader to open the envelope and discover what's inside.

### Tip #45          Pre-formatted Postcards

Many office supply stores and stationary catalogs have pre-formatted postcard designs.  They range from colored paper with borders, to photos of the world, money, or a handshake.  They come in sheets of 4 and are easily fed through your laser printer.  Cost is minimal: $7.00-$10.00 per hundred depending on the design and the supplier.  If you have a lot to say, purchase the "jumbo" 4x6 size.

### Tip #46          Announcements

Postcards are a fast, easy, economical way to make announcements to your customer base:

*Bob Smith has written an article appearing in this month's...*

*We have moved...*

*Now!  A toll-free number for your convenience.*

*Bob Smith will be appearing at _____.*

*Clearance!*

## Tip #47          Surveys

Need to accumulate some "research" for an article or speaking engagement? A postcard survey is easy to complete and takes virtually no time at all. Keep the questions and answers simple: yes/no; rank 1-5; put an x next to the top three... Mail to your customer base, or hand to customers when you see them and ask them to mail them back.

## Tip #48          Create Events

Use postcards to celebrate the number of years you've been in business.
> *Our 1st Anniversary celebration!*
> *Happy Birthday...to us!*
> *We're proud to have served the community for nine years.*

It's important to stay in touch with your client base as much as possible. Celebrating your yearly anniversary is a great reason to make contact.

## Tip #49          Custom Postcards

You can create a customized, full color, postcard just for your business. Include your logo, your picture, your company colors - all those things that make your company unique and recognizable. Use the custom postcard as you would the custom-designed newsletter.

## Tip #50          **"We've Missed You"**

Send a postcard to a customer you haven't seen for awhile, telling them they've been missed and you'd like to work with them again. Offer a "Welcome Back" discount.

A neat variation of this is to re-create the well known "While You Were Out" memo. Personalize it to the recipient's attention. Include your name, company name and phone number. Add a brief 2-3 line note to the bottom that says "We've missed you." And something that they have missed by not working with you recently (big sale, new technology, new offices). Be sure to check off the "please call" or "wants to see you" box.

# AUTHORING

### Tip #51        Leverage Your Expertise

Don't doubt your level of expertise by thinking, "Oh, everybody knows that". Everybody <u>does</u> <u>not</u> know what you know, and you'd be wise to leverage your expertise into profitable PR. Write a Top 10 List for your profession. Create an article titled, "Why _____ Never Works." Write an article that is contrary to popular belief at the moment, then you'll stand out from the crowd. You've spent years amassing your knowledge - use it in as many ways as possible.

### Tip #52        Professional Association Newsletters

Virtually every professional association has a monthly or bi-monthly newsletter. And since most of these organizations are strictly staffed by volunteers - they are desperate for any help they can get! Write an article or a series of articles. Ask that your photo be run with the article so that people will see you frequently and feel that they know you when they meet you in person.

## Tip #53          Trade and Professional Journals

You can develop a national reputation and gain credibility by publishing in the industry and trade journals of your profession. Here are a few keys to make this a successful endeavor:

♦ Contact each publication you wish to publish in and request their writer's guidelines. Follow the instructions exactly.

♦ Look through at least three years worth of back issues to get a feeling for the "tone" of the magazine, to see if the topic has already been addressed (although you can add a new twist), and to determine where your article might fit best (feature? monthly column?).

♦ Quote others as often as possible. The journals are not as likely to publish your opinion as they are to publish a collection of "expert" opinions. This is your article - you can quote only those people that support your opinion if you want - but don't make the article sound as though it is your personal soap box.

## Tip #54          Ghost Writing

Use your expertise to write someone else's material. You can gain as much exposure as a co-author or ghost writer as you can as an original author. It takes less creative work on your part since you are simply the organizer of the information and not the creator of it. Publicize your involvement with the work the same way you would publicize the authoring of your own work.

## Tip #55          Use an Editor

If you have not written a great deal, use an editor for the first few works. Your work will be easier to read and more likely to be used by the publications to which you are submitting. It is highly recommended that <u>you</u> fix your work after it comes back from the editor. If you have the editor fix it, you will continue to make the same mistakes. By using an editor and fixing your own work, you will learn correct technique and will eventually no longer need the editor.

## Tip #56          Self Publish Books

Depending on your product or service, a book is an excellent marketing tool. Books give you credibility as well as a side-line income to your regular business. Do not print more than 500 books. Your printer will convince you that it is more economical to print a larger number, but in the end, it's really not. You'll find that you have 2,500 sitting in your garage. Test the market first with a run of 500 or less. It <u>is</u> more economical to go back to the printer for future runs since all of the "set-up" work is done and paid for in the first printing.

## Tip #57          Internet Publishing

If you've thought of writing a weekly newspaper column - stop. Consider a weekly internet column instead. An internet column will gain you much wider exposure than your local newspaper and will allow you much more interaction with your audience. If you write something that is moving or thought provoking, you will find that a large number of your readers will contact you to further the discussion. You are now developing an e-mail mailing list of people who are interested in the things you write about.

# RADIO AND TV

## Tip #58          Talk About What You Know

There are more than 1,000 daily radio talk shows in the United States.  In addition, morning and drive time "personalities" frequently feature guests without classifying themselves as "talk shows." With the addition of morning and drive-time slots, the potential for radio appearances jumps to over 6,000 openings per day!  Surely you have something worthwhile enough to say that can fill 6-10 minutes.

## Tip #59          How to Find Radio Shows

Don't look for them - let them come to you.  There are a number of directories where you can list yourself as an expert on a certain topic.  Radio and television producers subscribe to these directories and, nine times out of ten, that is how they find their guests.   Two of the most beneficial directories to be listed in are *Radio and TV Interview Report* and *Yearbook of Experts, Authorities and Spokespersons.*

The *Yearbook* is a once-a-year directory.  *Radio and TV Interview Report* comes out three times a month and frequently runs special editions dedicated to a particular topic such as romance or health.  One of the attractions of *Radio and TV Interview Report* is that you can change your "pitch" frequently.

## Tip #60          Radio Contacts in Your Area

Many radio hosts will have you on as a guest simply because you are a local "celebrity."  To find out who to contact in your state, consult the *Gale Directory of Publishing and Broadcast Media* available at your local library, or check out Radio and Records on the Internet at www.rronline.com.  These two sources will also help you locate specific stations in other states if you choose to do a state-by-state media blitz.

## Tip #61          Radio Show Mailing Lists

Ingenious people, such as yourself, have already done the research for you.  If you wish to speed the process of finding radio shows, purchase a mailing list from one of the services that has compiled them.  One recommendation is Joe Sabah's list which is available on disk in a number of formats.  In addition, Joe includes *How to Get on Radio Talk Shows All Across America* As a bonus, Joe periodically sends an updated listed on disk.  It's well worth it to have Joe do the work for you!

## Tip #62       What to Say When You Get There

One way to quickly stop being a radio or television guest is to flop. The hosts
are looking for someone who is articulate and energetic. Three tips to being a
better guest:

1. Speak slowly and articulately. Speak in a relaxed manner, but not so
   relaxed that you are dropping the endings of words. Be aware of any verbal
   crutches you use such as "um," "well," or "you know."
2. Prepare a list of questions for the interviewer. Radio show hosts, especially,
   are doing twenty things at once. They greatly appreciate a list of questions
   that they can read that will make them sound as though they are quite
   familiar with you and your topic. An added benefit for you is that you are
   completely able to address the questions since you made them up!
3. Prepare a few amusing, interesting, or poignant stories, anecdotes, or
   quotes to illustrate your points. Although you may have a serious message
   to share, remember that the host's job is to entertain the audience and keep
   them tuned in.

## Tip #63       Create a Media Event

Local television news stations are always looking for "filler" stories. Create a
media event and invite the media. Make a donation of surplus goods to a local
charity. Sponsor a little league team or soap box derby competitor. Host an ice
cream social to kick off the junior high science fair. Think of an event that the
local media is likely to be intrigued by and want to share with their viewers.
Many times the local story is picked up by the national news affiliates of your
local station.

## Tip #64        Cable Access

Do your represent a product or service that has the potential for generating a lot of information or a lot of interest?  Local cable access stations are <u>always</u> looking for shows.  Watch a few shows on your local channel and look for contact information.  Write a brief proposal that states:

◆ The name of the show
◆ The purpose of the show
◆ The format (talk show, in-the-field reporting)
◆ What the value to the audience will be

Keep in mind that usually you will have to provide the crew for your show. Make sure you have enough friends to be camera operators and studio engineers.  The channel will teach you how to do it - but once you understand the process, they won't do it for you.


## Tip #65        Be Ready, Willing, and Able

If you are a popular guest, you will frequently receive requests to appear at unusual hours - 6:00 am or 12:00 midnight.  You'll also receive last minute requests when a scheduled guest cancels or your topic has become suddenly newsworthy.  Don't be finicky.  Say yes.  No PR is bad PR, as they say.

# OTHER GREAT IDEAS!

## Tip #66          Gift Certificates

Give gift certificates to your customers as holiday gifts. Use them to lure customers away from your competitors. Distribute them as anniversary gifts in thanks for your customer's patronage of the last year. Gift certificates can be purchased, pre-formatted and blank, from all office supply stores and paper catalogs.

## Tip #67          Motivational Words

When creating news releases or promotional items, there are a few words that generate immediate interest:
- free
- new
- win
- easy
- introducing
- save
- guaranteed

## Tip #68          PS

Research has shown, that when sending a direct mail letter, a PS at the bottom garners more attention than the entire body of the letter. If you are going to promote your business or services via letters of introduction to potential customers, make something up - anything - and include it in a PS

## Tip #69        Postage Paid Reply

Obtain a permit for Business Reply Mail from the post office ($85). Have cards pre-printed at a supply shop. You only pay for those cards that are *returned* - (postcards 22 cents and letters 34 cents). In addition you can set up an escrow account ($250) and the money you owe will be automatically deducted from the account.

## Tip #70        Fax back

Fax a compelling  message to your customer base with a reason for them to contact you - free report, 20% off to the first 12 respondents ... include a fax-back form that the customer can easily fill out and fax right back to you.

Add a "contest" twist:  "The funniest thing I heard this week," or "Where I'd prefer to be right now."  Have your fax back recipients return their entry by the end of the week and award a "valuable" prize.

## Tip #71        Broadcast Fax

Most computers come with built in fax/modems. You can create a promotional fax piece and set your computer up to fax it out over night to a large list of recipients. You don't have to be there to supervise the process. This will save you money (by utilizing the lower, night time phone charges) and free up your phone line during the day. Also, the fax will be there first thing in the morning when your customer arrives!

## Tip #72          Card Packs

You know those little cellophane packets you get every once in awhile that contain 40+ offers from different merchants?  Depending on the product or service you're selling, you may find that card packs impact your target market perfectly.  The next time you receive one, look through it for the "You, too, can advertise using cards packs!" information, or check out *The Business Publication Rates and Data Directory* which lists over 600 card packs.  Most major libraries carry this directory.

## Tip #73          Thank You Food

Who doesn't like food?  After landing a new client or contract, or completing a project, customers will appreciate a thank you of food.  Lovely gifts of chocolate can be found for under $10.00.  Fruit baskets or gourmet coffee baskets are also well received.  If your recipient is part of an office, it's a good idea to send something that can be placed in the community area so that all can share.  Also, keep in mind that many organizations forbid gifts over $50 in value.

## Tip #74          Custom Audio

If purchasing audio tapes as a give-away item, buy audio tape labels at any office supply store - print them on your own computer with "Compliments of: your name and company" and affix to the "B" side of the tape.

## Tip #75          Sponsor Your Own Community Event

Are you an avid golfer or basketball player?  Gather 20 of your friends together and create your own tournament.  Collect entry fees and donate a portion to the local boys and girls club, battered women's shelter, or hospice.  Be sure to get the local media to come and take pictures of you giving the check to the charity.

## Tip #76          Collaborate

Don't view your competitors as competitors - view them as collaborators.  What do you provide that they don't, and vice versa?  How can you help your customers by introducing them to your competitor and how can s/he do the same for you?  Do you need a shorter lead time than your competitor?  Can you provide smaller quantities or make house calls?  Work out a mutually beneficial agreement to provide those products or services that you cannot provide, but your competitor can.

## Tip #77          Create a Club

Is your product or service something that people will use frequently? Dry cleaner?  Video store?  Create a club that gives your customers a discount or a "prize" after a certain number of purchases or uses.  This keeps your customers coming back to you time and time again, and lessens their curiosity about your competitors wares because they are working toward something by staying with you.

## Tip #78　　　Flashback

Have a 50's, 60's or 70's celebration and roll your prices back to what they were, or would have been, during that decade. Market the event liberally.

## Tip #79　　　Unusual Advertising

Don't forget unusual sources of advertising: church bulletins, senior citizen newsletters, your health club or alumni newsletter. Frequently, you are able to place a monthly ad in these bulletins for less than $100 for the year!

## Tip #80　　　Urgent Information!

Send a mailing in the "urgent" envelopes that are available at stationary supply stores. They cost the same to mail* but appear to cost much more and appear to have urgency attached to them. They are typically 5x7 in size, made of card-stock, and are brightly colored - red, white, and blue; orange; yellow. They have phrases such as "Next Day Priority" and "Express Document Enclosed."

*Note: At the 5x7 envelope rate.

## Tip #81        Press Kit

A press kit is an organized, impressive way to make a statement about your product, service, or company. It doesn't have to be expensive, but it should look professional. Purchase folders with pockets at the office supply store. Include in the kit: any press releases, your bio, your photo, articles that have been written by you or <u>about</u> you, your brochure and marketing materials, fact sheets, testimonials, success stories, and miscellaneous items that will interest and educate the recipient.

Don't forget to include your business card and a short note that says, "I'll call you in a few days to make sure you've received this and to answer any questions you might have."

## Tip #82        Follow Up Calls

If you've sent a letter of introduction to a prospect, be sure to follow up with a phone call a few days later. A few days after the letter should have arrived, call the recipient and ask:

1. Did you receive the letter?
2. Did you have a chance to read it?
3. Do you have any questions?

This call allows you a few moments to establish a personal contact and get a feel for what their needs and concerns are.

## Tip #83        Pro Bono Work

Pro bono work is especially effective if you are in the business of selling information or services. Are you an accountant? Offer to audit the books of your professional association each year. Make sure that this service is noted and promoted in the association's literature. What better way to let hundreds of members know what it is that you do? Do you own a clothing store? Offer to coordinate or emcee a fashion show for the woman's club in your area. What can you do, effortlessly, that would be appreciated by others?

## Tip #84        Persistence

Persistence is key. Did you know that the typical sales pitch is ignored or rejected six times before the prospective client will make a purchase? Most uninitiated marketers give up after the first, second, or third attempt to contact a new customer.

## Tip #85        Accept Credit Cards

Depending on the product or service that you are marketing, credit cards can boost your sales by as much as 20%. Don't erroneously believe that people will not pay for professional services using a credit card. They will.

## Tip #86          Advertising

If you place ads in newspapers or magazines, be sure to vary the ad's content or angle frequently. A new ad will attract a different group of people each time it appears. An ad that says "Want to make $5,000 extra in the next 90 days?" will attract a different person than an ad that reads, "Want to Retire Early?" The product or service that you are pitching will be the same no matter who responds, but the way that you word the add will cause different people to respond.

## Tip #87          News Releases

Make sure that you have a headline that will attract the attention of the editor as well as the readers. Double space your press release and use the following margins:

  2" top
  1.5" left and right

The news release should answer the questions: who, what, where, when, why?

## Tip #88          Joint Mailings

If you are planning on a direct mail campaign to your customer base, search out a colleague - not a competitor - to share the mailing with you. You can fit four single sheets of 8.5 x 11 paper in an envelope for the same first class postage stamp. Why not send your information along with the information of a complimentary service or product? Bookstore/Video Store. Children's Clothing Store/Photographer. Writer/graphic artist.

## Tip #89        Vendor Malls/Trade Shows

Many professional associations hold a yearly showcase of their members and associated products and services. You do not have to be a member of the association to participate. Because they are locally produced, they are usually relatively inexpensive and allow you to make a person-to-person connection with your target market.

## Tip #90        Headshots

Depending on your product or service, and your ability to generate media and marketing attention, you may find that people ask for a headshot for publicity purposes. Have a headshot professionally done. Do not have your friend shoot your picture against a brick wall. A professional understands lighting and posing that translates into credibility for you.

## Tip #91        1-800 #

Toll free numbers are relatively inexpensive and appeal greatly to your customers. You only pay for the calls that come in, and a nominal monthly charge of less than $10.00 depending on your service provider. The number routes directly to your business phone line. You own your 800 number, so even if you switch service providers, your 800 number will stay the same (although you'll have to alert your new provider that you want them to host your 800 number also).

## Tip #92          1-800 #, cont.

The benefit of an 800 number is only realized if people actually use it! The directory assistance for 800 numbers (1-800-555-1212) does not automatically list your number like your local service provider automatically lists your home number in their directory. You must specifically request, from your service provider, that your number be listed with the 1-800 directory assistance.

## Tip #93          Stickers and Stamps

Stickers and stamps are a fast, efficient, eye-catching way to update your materials. Custom made stamps can be purchased at any office supply store from $4.00 - $25.00 depending on the number of lines necessary and the type style you choose. Stickers come in many shapes, sizes, and colors. Consider affixing a sticker or stamping a message to your stationary, envelopes, catalog, invoices, etc. Ideas: anniversary, reminder, thank you, new!, here's the information you requested.

## Tip #94          Rolodex Cards

Rolodex cards are inexpensive and unique. They can be printed on a thin plastic that is flexible and durable. The tab can be used to announce your name or profession. An excellent way to utilize rolodex cards is to put the words "Expert Source" on the tab and distribute to the media. The next time they have a question concerning your industry - you'll be sure to be quoted because you're an "Expert."

## Tip #95          Audio Tapes

Afraid your audience won't read your monthly newsletter? Consider taping it instead. There isn't a car sold today that doesn't include a cassette player, and people are <u>looking</u> for something to keep them awake and occupied during their daily commute. The audio should be short, 15-30 minutes and have some variety. An opinion, a summary of recent events in the industry, an interview with an expert in the field. And, of course, your contact information. Many small radio stations will allow you to use their production facilities in the evening or on weekends for a nominal fee.

## Tip #96          Warm Calls

Cold calls don't work. Have you ever bought insulation or windows over the phone? How many times have you been interrupted by someone attempting to sell you something? How did you feel about that person? Chances are that the person you call will feel that way toward you, too. However, warm calls are usually well received. A warm call follows an introduction or mailing.
"Hi Jim, this is Terry from _____. I recently sent you a package containing _____. Did you receive it?" (Nine out of ten people will say yes, even if they have no idea what you are talking about!) "Good. I won't interrupt your day, I just wanted to make sure that you saw _____."

## Tip #97          Logos

Logos are professional and memorable. Many printing companies have stock, or standard, logos that you may use on your business cards and stationary. Contact a graphic artist if you'd like one custom made for your business. Try the graphic arts department at the local university for an economical solution.

## Tip #98     Constant Contact

Constant contact is important. Try to find a reason to stay in touch with your clients and prospective clients at least quarterly. The old saying, "Out of sight, out of mind," is quite true. You will be amazed at the business that comes your way when you take the time to remind your clients and prospective clients of your existence.

## Tip #99     Constant Contact, cont.

Research has shown that mailing a series of letters two to three weeks apart can increase the rate of response.

## Tip #100     Endorsements

You can spend a lot of money on advertising and marketing and not accomplish much in the end. Why? Because paid advertising is paid advertising, and the customer knows that you're crowing about yourself. Endorsements, on the other hand, are basically word-of-mouth advertising from your previous clients. Ask your clients to write a short 2-3 line endorsement of your product or service that you can include in your marketing materials. Statements along the lines of, "Thanks to _____, I was able to _____." Or, "My _____ increased due to _____." End each endorsement with a vote of confidence: "I would highly recommend Chris' services."

## Tip #101     Guarantee Your Work

When people are hesitant to buy, a guarantee can help to alleviate their fears. Offering a "90-day No Questions Asked," or a "Lifetime Money Back Guarantee" allows people to try your product or service with peace of mind. Rarely, if ever, does a customer take advantage of the guarantee, and it is an excellent marketing technique. Especially if none of your competitors are offering one. "We are the only ____ to offer this guarantee!" is a powerful message.

> The real purpose of (this) book is to trap the mind into doing its own thinking.
> Christopher Morley

# Media and Marketing
# RESOURCES

## AUDIO CASSETTES

Amazon.com
    30,000 audio titles at 30% off
    www.amazon.com

Audio Books Direct
    317-541-8920

Audio-Tech Business Books
    800-776-1910

## CREDIT CARD MERCHANTS

NOVUS
    800-347-2000

## DATABASES / MAILING LISTS

ACT!  $189
    Symantec
    800-441-7234
    www.symantec.com

Alpha Five    $49
    Parsons Technology
    800-779-6000
    www.parsonstech.com

Avery Label Pro    $40
    800-252-8379

American Business Lists (broker)
    402-331-7169

PCS Mailing Lists (broker)
    800-532-5478

## DIRECTORIES

National Trade and Professional
Associations of the United States
    Columbia Books, Inc.
    1212 New York Ave., N.W.
    Suite 300
    Washington, DC 20005

Business Publication Rates and
Data Directory  (card packs)
    check your local library

Encyclopedia of Associations
    (ask for catalog)
    Gale Research Co.
    Book Tower
    Detroit, MI 48277-0748

## GIFT CERTIFICATES

Paper Direct
    800-272-7377

Viking
    800-421-4222

## GIFTS, GIMMICKS & GIVEAWAYS

Donut Boxes
    Jubilee Promotional Company
    800-851-1241
    www.donutbox.com

Successories®
    800-535-2773

Rolodex Cards
    Direct Promotions
    800-444-7706

Food
A Southern Season
    800-253-3663

"Urgent" Envelopes
    Tampa, FL
    800-795-2773
    ask for samples and price list

## INTERNET

For Web site creation or
domain name registration:
    Vision Technologies, Inc. (VTI)
    Phone: 1-800-644-6901
    E-mail: vti@vtinet.com
    Web site: www.vtinet.com

CompuServe
    800-848-8199

AngelFire
    www.anglefire.com

Hot Dog
    www.infoseek.com/Topic?tid=502&sv=N5&svx=nsiwebR1
    in the *Search for Shareware* box, type in: Hot Dog and click on Find
    you will be rewarded with 8 versions of Hot Dog, choose one for your skill level

## NEWSLETTERS (Software)

Microsoft Publisher®
    $89
    www.microsoft.com/products/

PrintShop Publishing Suite
    $69
    Parson's Technology
    800-779-6000
    www.parsonstech.com

Newsletters and More
    $29
    Parson's Technology
    800-779-6000
    www.parsonstech.com

## PHOTOS
Black & White Reproductions
JEM Photo
    412-621-0331
    $30/100, 4x5

## POSTCARDS

**Pre-formatted:**
Paper Direct
    800-272-7377

Viking
    800-421-1222

**Custom:**
US Press
    912-244-5634

Color for Real Estate
    800-221-1220
    (don't let the name fool you)

Web Cards www.printing.com

## RADIO/TV

Radio & Television Interview Report
800-989-1400 ext. 110

Yearbook of Experts, Authorities and
Spokespersons
2233 Wisconsin Ave. N. W.
Washington, DC 20007

Gale Directory of Publishing &
Broadcast Media
    3 volumes: best bet - local library
    Gale Research
    835 Penobscot Bldg.
    645 Griswold St.
    Detroit, MI 48226-4094

Radio and Records
    www.rronline.com

Joe Sabah's
Hot to Get on Radio & Talk
Shows All Across America
(and list of 700+ stations on disk)
    Jsabah@aol.com
    303-722-7200

## STICKERS

Viking
    800-421-1222

Interstate Label Co.
    800-426-3261

Stephen Fossler Co.
    800-762-0030